BRITISH PLANTS

Angela Royston

Heinemann
LIBRARY

First published in Great Britain by Heinemann Library
Halley Court, Jordan Hill, Oxford OX2 8EJ
a division of Reed Educational and Professional Publishing Ltd.

Heinemann is a registered trademark of Reed Educational & Professional Publishing Limited.

OXFORD   MELBOURNE   AUCKLAND
JOHANNESBURG   BLANTYRE   GABORONE
IBADAN   PORTSMOUTH NH   CHICAGO

Designed by AMR Ltd.
Printed and bound in Hong Kong/China by South China Printing Co. Ltd.

03 02 01 00
10 9 8 7 6 5 4 3 2 1

ISBN 0 431 00211 8

This title is also available in a hardback library edition (ISBN 0 431 00204 5)

British Library Cataloguing in Publication Data

Royston, Angela
  British plants. – (Plants)
  1. Plants – Great Britain – Juvenile literature
  I. Title
  581.9'41
  ISBN 0 431 00211 8

Acknowledgements
The Publishers would like to thank the following for permission to reproduce photographs:
Ardea: p9, J and S Bottomley p14, D Dixon p26, B Gibbons p10, P Morris p6; Bruce Coleman
Limited: A Davies p27; Garden and Wildlife Matters: pp4, 5, 7, 8, 11, 12, 17, 18, 19, 20, 22, 23,
24, 25, M Collins p21, J Hoare p15; Chris Honeywell: pp28, 29; Oxford Scientific Films:
D Brown p13; Tony Stone Images: T Latham p16.

Cover photograph: Garden and Wildlife Matters

The Publishers would like to thank Dr John Feltwell of Garden Matters for his
comments in the preparation of this book.

Every effort has been made to contact copyright holders of any material reproduced in this book.
Any omissions will be rectified in subsequent printings if notice is given to the Publisher.

Any words appearing in bold, **like this**, are explained in the Glossary.

Contents

Where plants grow

Plants grow all over Britain in many
different places. They grow in woods,
fields, gardens, moors and even between
the stones in a wall.

All plants need water and sunlight to grow. Some plants grow best in one kind of place, while others, such as dandelions, grow almost everywhere.

Wasteground

Sometimes a piece of land is cleared, but the wind blows **seeds** onto it. **Weeds** begin to grow on the bare land and soon produce **flowers**.

Before long, their seeds are growing too, and more seeds are blown in or dropped by birds. This wasteland is now covered with plants!

Woodland flowers

Plants need sunlight, but woods are dark and shady in summer. Many woodland plants **flower** in spring before the trees have many leaves.

Some woodland flowers grow from
bulbs. A bulb is a store of food which
the plant uses until its own leaves
begin to make food.

Ferns and mosses

Ferns and mosses like damp, shady places and so they grow well in woods, even in summer. Ferns and mosses do not produce **flowers** to make **seeds**.

Instead they produce millions of tiny **spores**, which blow in the wind and start to grow on new ground. Moss grows on trees and even on stones.

Hedges

A hedge provides a home for many kinds of plants and animals. Climbing plants such as wild roses grow up other plants to get more light.

Plants that prefer more shade, shelter among the **roots** and **stems** near the ground.

Roadsides

The sides of motorways and railways can be a good place for plants to grow. Trains and traffic roar past, but no-one picks the **flowers**.

Wild flowers grow well on many
kinds of banks and roadsides. They
get plenty of light and some shelter
from the wind.

Fields and meadows

Meadows are grassy fields where sheep and cattle often graze. The animals nibble the grass and cut it short, but some **flowers** still manage to grow.

Thistles have sharp prickles which put the animals off. Daisies have flat leaves which are too close to the ground for the animals to eat.

Marshes

Marshes are very wet for all or most of the year. Many kinds of rushes and reeds grow tall in the wet soil.

These colourful marsh marigolds grow in wet fields as well as on the banks of streams and ditches.

Growing in water

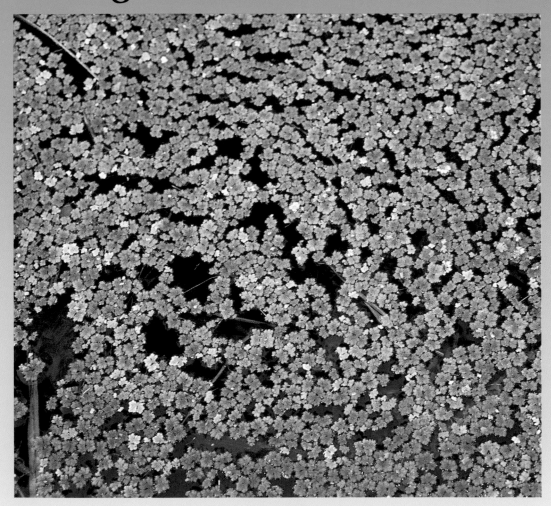

Some water plants just float on the surface of the water. Other water plants grow **roots** in the mud at the bottom of the pond.

This little frog has climbed onto the shiny flat leaf of a water-lily. The water-lily **flower** has thick tough petals to keep the water out.

Seaside

Plants that grow by the sea have to put up with strong winds and salty spray. This clump of sea pinks is firmly rooted between the rocks.

Marram grass grows well on sandy dunes although the sand is loose and dry. Its long **roots** and leaves stop the sand blowing away.

Seaweeds

Seaweeds grow in shallow water
where the plants still get light from the
sun. Some seaweeds are left high and
dry at **low tide**.

They have thick slimy skins to stop them drying out and dying. Most seaweeds float in the water, but some cling to stones and rocks.

Heaths, moors and bogs

Gorse, heather and rough grass grow well on heaths and moors. Heaths are often quite dry, but many moors are wet and boggy.

The soil in some bogs is so poor that only plants like the sundew can grow there. Sundews catch insects to eat to make up for the poor soil.

Catching seeds

Find out what **seeds** are scattered by the wind. In summer or autumn, put a **grease band** in the middle of an empty patch of garden.

After a week, examine it with a
magnifying glass. How many different
kinds of seeds have blown onto it?

Plant map

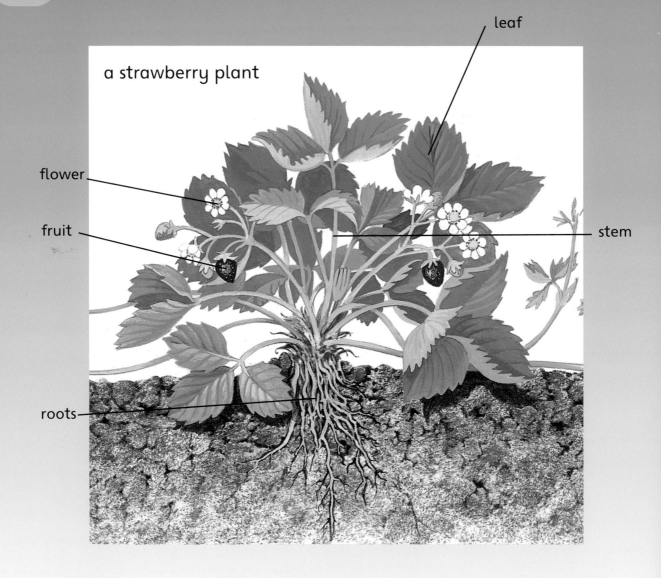

a strawberry plant

leaf

flower

fruit

stem

roots

Glossary

bulb	swollen root which contains a store of food. Plants which grow from bulbs die back after flowering but grow again the following year.
flower	the part of a plant which makes new seeds
grease band	strips of sticky paper which can be bought from a plant nursery or garden shop
low tide	when the sea is at its lowest
marsh	land which is partly covered with water for most of the year
roots	parts of a plant which take in water, usually from the soil
seed	contains a tiny plant before it begins to grow and a store of food
spore	the cell from which a new fern, moss or fungus begins to grow
stem	The part of a plant from which the leaves and flowers grow
weed	wild flowers which grow and form new seeds very quickly

Index